WILL

I

BE

IN

HEAVEN?

By

Glenn Adams

All scripture quotations, unless otherwise indicated, are taken from the King James Version of the Holy Bible.

Why I Wrote This Book

This book is for everyone that is unsure of the answer to the question – Will I Be In Heaven? Far too many people, when posed with that question respond with, "I hope so".

I want you to know so!

This is a short read that will clear up any misconceptions. Hint - It has nothing to do with being Good!

Chapter 1

Will I be in Heaven?

If you are like most people, you have asked yourself this question before – maybe many times. If you are like some people, you already know the answer. If you are like many people, you aren't sure. People are asked this question on the street and in surveys. Did you know that when people are asked if they will be in Heaven, the number one response is, "I hope so"?

I don't know about you but I find that to be very troubling! When asked about something as important as where you will spend eternity, I want you "to know so." I don't want you to have to wonder or doubt. That's why this book is for you. When you finish this book, there will be no confusion. You will know the answer to that question..... Will I be in Heaven?

So, let's get started at the very beginning.

When we come into this world, we come in as curious, inquisitive creatures. We begin gaining knowledge and information the moment we are born and that continues for the rest of our lives. For the purpose of this book we will limit our discussion, for obvious reasons, to the spiritual knowledge we have gained. Make sense?

Have you ever wondered where you came from? Ever wondered where this earth, sun, moon and stars came from? Ever wondered if there really is a Heaven or Hell, or even a God? Ever wondered who gets to go to Heaven? Of course you have! We all have! That's normal and natural.

If you are like most people, you have already formed opinions about these things. The question is, which opinions or beliefs are right and what are they based on? Are your beliefs based on what someone told you whether it was a family member, friend, or even a church leader? It's sad to say but most form their beliefs from street talk or influences and opinions of those who are at best misguided.

There are those who believe or say they believe there is no God. I don't believe you fall into that category simply because you are reading this book.

The purpose of this book is to simply help guide those who have a genuine desire for truth and want to make the right decision about their eternal destiny.

We are going to look at what many believe, but we are going to also look at God's word and see how accurate those beliefs are. God's word – The Holy Bible – is the standard to determine which beliefs are true and accurate and which aren't. You are definitely reading the right book!

Chapter 2

There may be as many opinions about how to go to Heaven as there are people. Here are a few of the most popular ones:

1.Whoever believes in God will go to Heaven.

2.Whoever goes to church will go to Heaven.

3.Whoever obeys the Ten Commandments will go to Heaven.

4.Whoever does more good things than bad things will go to Heaven.

These opinions may seem OK, but they are all wrong.

Let's break each one of the four down and just look at them with a little common sense. Obviously the ones who give these answers haven't really spent much time seriously thinking about Heaven and how to get there, much less done any research.

The first one is whoever believes in God will go to Heaven. This opinion is wrong for several reasons: The Bible never states that believing in God will get you into Heaven, and confirms that such is the case in *James 2:19 - Thou believest that there is one God; thou doest well: the devils also believe, and tremble.*

Satan (the Devil) believes God exists. In fact, he talks with God in Job chapters 1 and 2. Yet, he is not going to Heaven—he is going to be cast into the lake of fire and brimstone (hell). This is recorded in Revelation chapter 20, verse 10. Angels that sinned were cast into hell—and they knew God. Read 2 Peter, chapter 2, verse 4.

Sorry, believing in God is not enough to allow you to enter Heaven.

Now the second opinion or belief is that whoever goes to church will go to Heaven. Once again, the Bible never states that going to church will get you into Heaven. What if you attended a church that doesn't even go by the Bible or one that twists everything in the Bible. How would you ever know you weren't part of a cult or false religion?

Sorry, going to church will not get you into Heaven.

Okay, let's look at the next one. Whoever obeys the Ten Commandments will go to Heaven. Now this is one to really step back and think about. Many religions are centered around this. If you really believe that keeping the Ten Commandments gets someone into Heaven, then stop and think for a minute and name one person that you know that has kept all Ten Commandments. See, you can't because even the best, even the most moral of all people have broken most if not all the commandments.

James 2:10 - For whosoever shall keep the whole law, and yet offend in one point, he is guilty of all.

Also understand the Bible never states that obeying the Ten Commandments will get you into Heaven.

People who examine themselves truthfully discover they have broken most of the Ten Commandments at some time in their lives—and if you break one – you are guilty of breaking them all.

So, that leaves us with the last of our top beliefs which is whoever does more good things than bad things will go to Heaven.

This is probably the most common of all the wrong beliefs for many reasons. The Bible never states that doing more good things than bad things will get you into Heaven.

Let's just ask ourselves some questions and see if this makes any logical or rational sense.

More good things than bad things? Really? Who will keep score? Yourself?

Who or what determines what is good things and what is bad? What standard will you go by?

Do you just have to have one more good thing than bad?

What if you die today and you are presently behind in the score by one or two.

Do you see how ridiculous this line of reasoning is?

So now that you are seeing that what many people believe is incorrect just from a logic standpoint, let's lay for you the proper foundation to help you make the right decision and know that your eternal destiny is secure. Let's start that proper foundation with faith.

Chapter 3

The first area I want you to look at is faith. Faith is not a one- time decision, but rather an ongoing one. Faith will be a part of your life forever whether you consider yourself spiritual or not.

Just what exactly is faith? The dictionary defines faith as 1) complete trust or confidence, 2) system of religious belief, 3) belief in religious doctrines.

My personal paraphrase definition of faith is anything that you believe in that can't be explained using your five senses – see, smell, hear, taste, and feel. The Bible tells us in *Hebrews 11:1 that faith is the substance of things hoped for, the evidence of things not seen.*

Have you ever heard someone described as a person of faith? What they do not realize is that everyone is a person of faith in something! We all use faith every day. Think about it. When is the last time you examined a chair for sturdiness before you sat down in it? Probably never. You just believed and trusted that it would hold you up. That is using faith.

I also want you to understand that faith is like your muscles. The more you use your muscles, the larger they get. It's the same with faith. You have to exercise your faith as well for it to grow.

Usually related to the topic of faith is religion and that is what we are going to look at next.

Chapter 4

Religion is defined as 1) A set of beliefs concerning the cause, nature, and purpose of the universe, especially when considered as the creation of a superhuman agency or agencies, usually involving devotional and ritual observances, and often containing a moral code governing the conduct of human affairs. 2) A specific fundamental set of beliefs and practices generally agreed upon by a number of persons or sects.

Notice what the first part of the first definition says – a set of beliefs concerning the cause, nature, and purpose of the universe.

Another dictionary defines religion as a belief in a personal God or Gods.

I don't know about you, but I believe in a personal God. I believe in one God and I believe He is the creator of this universe. These are choices that I made based on faith.

Faith and religion are considered somewhat synonymous. They both have to do with our beliefs. As a matter of fact I think we can come to the conclusion that we are all "persons of faith" and "religious". It's just that we may differ on what that faith is in or what that religion is about.

Actually everyone is religious in the sense that they have a god. Did you know that whoever or whatever is the most important thing to you in your life is your god! That could be a person, house, job, game, television, money, clothes, iPad, iPod, cell phone, or even yourself. Uh oh! Did I strike a nerve there? I'm sure I did with some of you. That's okay as long as you get the message.

I know that some of you are turned off by religion mainly because you believe that it is nothing but a bunch of rules and regulations, or commandments or laws that you have to follow, (which you interpret to mean you're not allowed to have any fun). You know what? In many cases you're right. That's exactly what "religion" is – rules, laws, commandments, and rituals. I don't want you to follow a religion but I do want you to know what religion is!

A religion is formed when people take the Bible and add to it or change it by incorporating their own opinions, beliefs and rituals to it.

In the Bible, during Old Testament times, the people were given the 10 Commandments and the Levitical law (ceremonial law) to live by. If they kept the law and commandments they were blessed.

If not, they were cursed. That was the case in Old Testament times. Read Deuteronomy chapter 28 and you will see all the blessings and cursings. They didn't understand that the law was there to show them that they couldn't keep the law. It was a "mirror" and still is today, to show us how unrighteous we are and that we need a savior.

Now what I have just described to you in essence is religion – rules, laws, rituals and commandments! That was the old covenant made through Moses to the children of Israel.

That leads us to the next topic that I want to make sure you understand – Christianity and the Gospel of the Grace of God!

Chapter 5

Some people consider Christianity a religion. Most Christians however don't because it is not about how well we perform laws, commandments or rituals. It is all about our faith and belief in the person of Jesus Christ and what He has done for us. Do you see the difference in that from what you just read about religion? Christianity is all about what Jesus did for us at the cross and our faith and trust in Him, whereas religion is all about us and how well we are performing the rules, laws, or commandments. Instead of our faith and focus being on ourselves and our performance, our focus is on Jesus and what He did for us, or at least, it should be.

Being good is not what saves you! Did you know that sins are not the cause of someone going to Hell? No, its unbelief and rejection of Jesus Christ that does. Many people are misled about this so I am going to explain it thoroughly for you. Even some Christians are confused about what the Christian life is all about. I know I was! That is why I am going into much detail about this because I don't want any of you mixed up. Salvation is foundational to the rest of your life so therefore I want you to be completely clear.

Growing up, my understanding of the Christian life was that you lived at the church. It seemed as though we were always there. Sunday school, preaching, training union, preaching, prayer meeting, preaching, mama's WMU meetings, preaching, daddy's deacons meetings, preaching, R.A.'s, you name it – we were there. Oh, I forgot visitation. Well, I began to resent it! It got to where my favorite part of every meeting or service was the benediction.

Not only did I dread all the meetings and services, I dreaded the preparation. We had this ritual that we went through on Saturday evenings. After supper we had to get ready for – you guessed it – church! That meant we had to study our Sunday school lesson, fill out that little white envelop for our tithe, shine our shoes, and get our clothes ready. Now shining my shoes was quite a chore. You see, I only had one pair and by the time Saturday evening rolled around, they looked like they had been through three world wars! I almost needed to putty them before I shined them.

The clothes situation wasn't any better. I had an older brother so that meant I had to wear all his hand-me-downs. If I ever got a new suit, my mother would buy it so that it would fit me three years later. "You'll grow into it," she said. I don't remember ever growing into any of those clothes. I was as rough on my clothes as I was my shoes. I'm sure they were worn out long before they ever fit.

And then there was this wool suit. This was in the days before they began putting a lining in wool. It itched so badly. It felt like a terrible case of poison ivy. I was miserable! I will never forget one Sunday at church my mother looking down at my feet and saying, "What are you wearing?" I looked down and my pajama bottoms were sticking out from under my pants. I had ingeniously figured out if I wore those under my pants they wouldn't itch so badly. Who knows, maybe I invented lined wool clothes!

I obviously had an immature, distorted view of what Christianity was all about. To me, growing up, it all boiled down to how well a person performed or how well they were keeping the rules, laws, and commandments. I didn't comprehend or understand my relationship with Jesus. I understood rules and rituals. I don't want that to be the case for you.

Christianity (being a Christian) is not about being good or bad. It is not about being perfect little goody two shoes. It is not about following a list of rules or procedures or laws or rituals. It is not a bunch of thou shalts or thou shalt nots. It is not something to keep you from having fun. It's not a lot of "have-to's".

If you recognize that you do things wrong and have done things wrong in the past (committed sins) then you recognize that you are a sinner and need a savior. The Bible tells us that all (that means everyone) has sinned and we are all guilty. We cannot be "good enough" to earn our way to Heaven. We cannot be perfect. Jesus is the only one that has ever been perfect, and kept the whole law and when you realize this, then you can understand why we need a savior and why that savior has to be Jesus! He kept the whole law on our behalf. He fulfilled it! When we accept Jesus as our savior, God looks at us as being perfect because he sees us through the shed blood of his only son.

God made it so simple to become a Christian that even a little child could understand it. It's all in this verse in *Acts 16:31, "Believe on the Lord Jesus Christ and you will be saved."* Period. End of sentence. Christ died for our sins, was buried, and He rose from the grave on the third day. If you believe this you will be saved.

Christianity is a "relationship" with a person, and that person is Jesus Christ. Stop and think for a minute. Christians have a relationship with, and worship a "risen", "resurrected", "living" savior. This is the primary reason that makes Christianity different from "religions."

I trust that you see that being a Christian is not "religion" but a relationship. Doing things (works or good deeds) does not save you. Going to church does not, reading the Bible does not, getting sprinkled or baptized does not, teaching a Bible class does not, being in ministries at church does not, and even being a pastor does not. Only your belief does!

Our works do not save us, but once we believe, we end up doing good works because that is what is in our heart to do. We have a desire to. God gives us a whole new set of taste buds!

Ephesians 2:10 - For we are his workmanship, created in Christ Jesus unto good works, which God hath before ordained that we should walk in them.

Let me explain it this way. Being saved or becoming a Christian is like getting a heart transplant. The Bible says in John 3:7 that you must be born again. *2Corinthians 5:17 says if any man be in Christ, he is a new creature: old things are passed away; behold, all things are become new.* God transforms our heart and we are born again spiritually!

Many of you have already made the decision to become Christians, and I congratulate you and praise the Lord for you and the choice you have made. You will see that even as Christians we still face difficult situations and circumstances. I know; I've been there. But, if you have Christ in your heart, you will learn how to deal with anything this old world or Satan will throw at you.

Some of you have not accepted Jesus as your savior and Lord. That's okay. Maybe you are just trying to understand what being a Christian is. Maybe you are just trying to find out how to get to Heaven. I hope your questions and curiosities are becoming clear by now. This book will help you understand how to build the proper foundation for your life. Construction begins with salvation.

Maybe a family member or friend has asked you to read this. That's okay too. That means they care very deeply for you and want you to have the very best that life has to offer. And, that comes with the Christian life.

Being saved means that you get to go to Heaven. Being saved means that you have the Holy Spirit living within you. Being saved means that you have a personal relationship with Jesus Christ. Being saved means that you can live an abundant life, if you choose to, while you are here on this earth. But, that doesn't mean you won't face challenges!

The most important decision you will ever make in your entire lifetime is to accept Jesus Christ as your Lord and Savior. Why? Because that determines not only your eternal destination, but also the quality of life you will live while still on this earth! Trust me......it's a choice you will never regret. Everything else hinges on this.

Jesus loves each and every one of us so much. He loves you that much! Would you like to know for sure that you are going to Heaven to spend eternity with Him? Would you like to have a close personal relationship with the One who loves you so much He was willing to die for you and longs to live with you? Of course you would - who wouldn't want to have that?

I invite you and encourage you to make that decision right now if you haven't. Just simply say, "Dear God, I know and believe that you love me and that you sent your only begotten son, Jesus Christ, to die for my sins, that he was buried and on the third day he arose from the grave. I thank you that you have forgiven me of my sins and I ask you to come into my life right now and save me. Help me to live the rest of my life for you. In Jesus name I pray, amen." If you just prayed that prayer and were sincere then you are now saved and will live forever.

Congratulations!!!

Chapter 6

Let's go just a little deeper here to help you understand the differences between Christianity and other faiths or beliefs.

A crucial distinction about Christianity is that God cared enough about humankind to reach down and compassionately provide a way for us to be in a right relationship with Him. In other religions, people vainly attempt to reach God and earn their own salvation by doing good deeds and by refraining from bad behavior.

The problem for those people is that no one can ever be good enough to earn his own salvation. In other words, no one can ever reach God through his own efforts. That is why God made a way for us by sending His Son Jesus to live a holy and sinless life and suffer the payment for our sins. In this way, if we believe in Jesus and choose to follow

Him, we are forgiven by God and given new life.

Another critical difference is that in Christianity people can truly have genuine assurance of their salvation. They can be certain that they are going to Heaven because their salvation is anchored in what Jesus already did for them. As a result, Christians have peace in their hearts about where they will go when their lives on earth are finished.

In other faiths, people cannot be assured that they will go to Heaven because they can never know if they have done enough good works to earn God's favor or forgiveness. They have to continually try to earn their salvation—even until their last day and dying breath. They cannot experience the restful assurance that God gives those who trust in Jesus Christ.

I trust that this may clear up any misconceptions that some of you may have.

Now let me share with you a little more about my Christian life.

Chapter 7

I must confess something to you. My Christian life has not always been smooth sailing. Although I was saved at a very young age, and knew that Jesus was my Savior, I didn't make him Lord of my life. I chose to continue to do things my way and the world's way, rather than God's way. What a mistake! Can any of you relate to this? I didn't really understand how to live by grace rather than condemnation. Because of that, my Christian life in many ways has been more of a roller coaster ride, with many ups and downs. One of the things that I had misunderstood is in this verse:

Galatians 2:16

Knowing that a man is not justified by the works of the law,

*but by the faith of Jesus Christ, even we
have believed in Jesus Christ,*

*that we might be justified by the faith of
Christ, and not by the works of the law:*

*for by the works of the law shall no flesh
be justified.*

I didn't know about this verse growing up. I
thought I was justified or accepted
according to my behavior.

What this verse means is that God is more
interested in your "heart" than He is your
"behavior". He knows that if your heart is
right, then your behavior will be right. We
have this tendency, even as Christians, to
focus on the behavior and start condemning
rather than looking at the heart and
transforming.

I am so thankful that I finally learned this,
even though it took many years.

My prayer is that you will learn who you are in Christ, will live by grace and not the law (condemnation), will know how to deal with the issues you face, will choose to live the abundant and victorious life, and will join with me in being a true soldier of Jesus Christ!

So now I ask you – Will you be in Heaven? You can now answer that question without saying "I hope so".

I pray that this book has been as much of a blessing to you reading it as it has been for me in writing it.

EPILOGUE

These are some scriptures that will be very helpful for you to help understand and solidify your foundation as a Christian.

Isaiah 53:6 All we like sheep have gone astray; we have turned every one to his own way; and the LORD hath laid on him the iniquity of us all.

John 1:12 But as many as received him, to them gave he power to become the sons of God, even to them that believe on his name:

John 3:16 For God so loved the world, that he gave his only begotten Son, that whosoever believeth in him should not perish, but have everlasting life.

John 3:17 For God sent not his Son into the world to condemn the world; but that the world through him might be saved.

John 17:3 And this is life eternal, that they might know thee the only true God, and Jesus Christ, whom thou hast sent.

Acts 2:21 And it shall come to pass, that whosoever shall call on the name of the Lord shall be saved.

Acts 4:12 Neither is there salvation in any other: for there is none other name under Heaven given among men, whereby we must be saved

Acts 15:11 But we believe that through the grace of the Lord Jesus Christ we shall be saved,

Acts 16:30-31 And brought them out, and said, Sirs, what must I do to be saved? And they said, Believe on the Lord Jesus Christ, and thou shalt be saved, and thy house.

Romans 3:23 For all have sinned, and come short of the glory of God;

Romans 5:8 But God commendeth his love toward us, in that, while we were yet sinners, Christ died for us.

Romans 5:9-10 Much more then, being now justified by his blood, we shall be saved from wrath through him. For if, when we were enemies, we were reconciled to God by the death of his Son, much more, being reconciled, we shall be saved by his life.

Romans 6:23 For the wages of sin is death; but the gift of God is eternal life through Jesus Christ our Lord.

Romans 10:9-10 That if thou shalt confess with thy mouth the Lord Jesus, and shalt believe in thine heart that God hath raised him from the dead, thou shalt be saved. For with the heart man believeth unto righteousness; and with the mouth confession is made unto salvation.

Romans 10:13 For whosoever shall call upon the name of the Lord shall be saved.

1 Corinthians 15:1-4

1 Moreover, brethren, I declare unto you the gospel which I preached unto you, which also ye have received, and wherein ye stand;

2 By which also ye are saved, if ye keep in memory what I preached unto you, unless ye have believed in vain.

3 For I delivered unto you first of all that which I also received, how that Christ died for our sins according to the scriptures;

4 And that he was buried, and that he rose again the third day according to the scriptures:

2 Corinthians 5:17 Therefore if any man be in Christ, he is a new creature: old things are passed away; behold, all things are become new.

Ephesians 2:8-9 For by grace are ye saved through faith; and that not of yourselves: it is the gift of God: Not of works, lest any man should boast.

1 John 1:9 If we confess our sins, he is faithful and just to forgive us our sins, and to cleanse us from all unrighteousness.

1 John 4:19 We love him, because he first loved us

1 John 5:11-13 And this is the record, that God hath given to us eternal life, and this life is in his Son. He that hath the Son hath life; and he that hath not the Son of God hath not life. These things have I written unto you that believe on the name of the Son of God; that ye may know that ye have eternal life, and that ye may believe on the name of the Son of God.

Contact Information

Email –
glennadamsatrightlydividing@gmail.com

Other Books by Glenn Adams

Rightly Dividing the Word of God

Living The Christian Life Without Laws, Commandments and Condemnation

Childrens Books by Glenn and Tammy Adams

Family Bible Coloring Book for Kids

All books available at Amazon